James Adams

A Black Man's Journey Out of Homelessness in Puyallup, WA

Written in collaboration by James Adams, Chuck Fitzgerald, Alan Woody

This book is dedicated to anyone
who has suffered or been

persecuted in this world

CHAPTER ONE: THE 1960'S

In the Year of our Lord, 1961, a baby was born in East St. Louis, IL to a black skin mother.   He was named James Adams.   Along with St. Louis Missouri, East St. Louis is a city that became the harbinger in the 1940's and 1950's for thousands of black and brown skin people, escaping the north and the south, who were tired of being dirt poor. For several years life was good for them.   They had decent paying jobs and families supported each other.   However, the 1960's was a harsh time for Illinois cities that were inhabited predominately by black and brown skin people.

The downtown businesses were burned during the "riots" which followed President John F. Kennedy's, and then five years later, Dr. Martin Luther King, and Attorney General Robert F. Kennedy's assassination. Those cities and many others throughout the United States during the 1960's were devastated economically and socially. Those cities looked like Beirut and the bombed out cities in the Middle East from years of hatred and war.

This baby would grow up in one of the most degraded and devastated cities in the Midwest. He was in an environment which was detrimental to and for the educational system in the city.   Learning to read and write was an anomaly for city children.   The city school systems had very little tax base from which to generate enough money to conduct the challenge of creating and perpetuating a learning situation, for any of the thousands of children who were locked within the holds of poverty and desperation.

Meanwhile the outlying suburbs of these cities prospered.   The white skin people began to move out of the cities as fast as the real estate scammers could build shitty quality, ticky-tack houses and sell them for way too much money.   White people were scared and willing to pay those prices just to escape the turmoil and darkness of the cities.

As soon as these suburbs could be established as towns and villages, they began to draw up laws and rules prohibiting anyone who had a skin color other than lily-white buying houses in their neighborhoods.   And God bless the person of Jewish faith who attempted to secure a bank loan to purchase a home in those suburbs. There was no way in hell that even if "those people" had hard cold cash, that they could buy real estate.   There were many vague and non-valid reasons to deny the sale of homes to them.

Life was good in the small towns in rural America during those days. The schools I attended through my childhood contained not one child "of color".   When my parents moved me to the small southeast Missouri town of four thousand people, just before I started the third grade, there were signs on the side of the highways at the town limits that said "Welcome to The Town Of Dexter.   A Small Town With Friendly People".   And at the bottom of that sign it was written in capital letters", "COLOREDS TO BE OUT OF TOWN BEFORE SUNSET".   As a child I could not grasp the implications of the sign, but I never have forgotten seeing it.

  I'm not sure what year the new signs were installed, but they did not have that warning posted on them.

CHAPTER TWO: IN TOTAL CONTRAST

That black baby born in East St. Louis grew up in the harshest possible environment. By the age of ten he was standing on the street corners holding heroin and speed and downers for the dealers and pimps standing twenty feet behind him watching and counting. This child learned quickly how to recognize and count money even though he struggled to write his own name. He could not read the words on the bills but he could damned- well read the numbers! Surrounded by whores and drug addicts he was able to earn a couple of bucks so that he could survive on the street.   Needless to say, that child grew into a young man who only knew the "street" and eventually was apprehended, convicted, and imprisoned.   By that time he had sold illicit chemicals in Chicago and Detroit and various other cities.   He wore the finest silk clothes and shoes shinny and hats tall and long black coats.   Chains of gold and silver and teeth skins of gold were the everyday trappings of "Papa G". Rolls of hundreds and change rattled in his pockets.   He was a man of "street status" and savvy. For twelve years he sat in cells and cleaned and swept hallways and washed windows and mirrors. He ate at the crowded tables and

witnessed the cruelty of the masses
who were forced to prey one upon
the other.   He served in the
State Penitentiary system twelve
long and sad years.
During those same years I, on the
other hand, lived in total comfort
and safety.   I finished high school,
serving as 'Student Council
President' my senior year.   I
enrolled in college and began my
life of adulthood.   I worked in high
school and college so that I could
maintain an automobile and keep
some "go-to hell" money in my
pockets.   I did have a savings and
checking account at the bank across
the street from the service station
where I worked half days as a junior
and senior.   I never remember
going to bed hungry.   I always had

good health care and shelter, and
plenty of clothing and warm coats
and shoes and spending money.
Enough for any child.   Needing
nothing.   Being held and loved and
coddled and hugged.   I truly was a
child of white privilege.
I married my last year of college
and finished my degree.   For two
kids with degrees, fresh out of
college and serving in their first
'real' job, life could get no better!

CHAPTER THREE: PUYALLUP

At the age of fifty-two a misguided man found himself in the great state of Washington. He had landed in a small outlying city of Seattle which had started as a farming community in colonial times. He was one of a very few black skin people in the county. He was a black man in a white man's world. He had little money and he had hooked up with a lady of his fancy, Robin, along the way. She did have a monthly disability check which was barely enough money to support one person for a couple of weeks. They had no housing, no transportation except for a bicycle, and no savings. Therefore they lived on the streets and in the available shelters.   The town had a "program" called 'Freezing Nights' which was a project of seven local churches. Their goal was to feed and shelter as many vagabonds as possible. They rotated the program from church to church from November through March.   God bless the righteous people of Puyallup.   I still haven't figured out what a Puyallup is.   It is obvious to me that it is a Native American word, but what the hell is a puyallup? They went through the lunch line at a participating church one cold, wet day and was served a ladle of pork-and-beans as he went along the line.   After he sat down and ate his meal the bean server came to his table and struck up a conversation.   This conversationalist was interested in the whole concept of living on the street.   He was an artist and a local hero of modest recognition.   He was a true humanitarian as are artist everywhere.   This middle-aged artist of Irish blood and this lost, lonely, poor, middle-aged man of black skin, formed a bond in only a few minutes.   The artist could not stop thinking about James's condition and situation.   They met again in the food line and set up a time to "get together" and discuss possible solutions to his many problems.   The rest is history!

But since you do not know that bit
of history, allow me to continue
with this story. The red haired artist
of local acclaim needed a cause to
take up.   He was bored and had
plenty of time on his hands.   He
was not one to sit on his laurels.   A
school teacher of many productive
years.   A recognized speaker of
local fundraising gatherings which
included Mayors and Counsel
People.   People who loved to
contribute to and sponsor local
charities.   The rich and
want-to-be's.   He was a legend in
his own mind.
The world of the black man so
foreign and novel to this white man
of privilege, was in his mind
inconceivable and impenetrable.
Therefore set the challenge.   The

mountain unclimbed. The crux uncrossed.   The trail untraveled. The number unused.   This white man gathered all of his courage and fortitude and blasted into the great unknown.   He made a rational decision to take on the burdens of a man with a woman hanging on. He dusted his broom and walked into the realm of undeniably.   The world of no return.   He took upon himself a mantle of search and destroy.   Of finders keepers losers weepers.   Out for blood.   Out to win.   Once you cross that bridge, you lose control.   You are out in the rain.   Out in the shadows of the lost.   Those who have no past, no future, no dreams, no wishes, no feelings of happy redemption.

So this man, the artist, the humanitarian, asked a simple question of this ex-con of despicable behavior, sitting across the table with his lover in tow. "What would like to do with your life from this point forward"? Who knows the answer to that question, not me.   The bond that had happened and the overwhelming need to help a person, solidified the future.   Well within the bounds of freedom and the unknown, the story continues. The lives of people unknown and distant.   Waiting in the wings of humanity.   This man who served 12 years in prison and paid his dues.   He had spent a lifetime wandering through the courts and proclaiming his repentance.   His absolution.   Promising to never repeat the dastardly deeds of his past.

CHAPTER FOUR: THE STRUGGLE

The artist agreed to give James and his lady a ride to Tacoma the following day.   They were going to look at an apartment there.   He met them at McDonalds' the next day and they embarked on their journey.   As they drove he casually asked them if they had Washington state identification, money, and references. James told him they did not. Explaining that these were basic requirements for renting an apartment he turned the car around and took them back to McDonalds' and dropped them off.   He got their cell number and told them he

would call and arrange to meet
again to see if he could help them
work out these problems.
James had been out of prison three
years by then and had wandered
around with no identification.   He
had a strong desire to "go straight".
  He had kept his "nose clean" but
as one can imagine he had been
stopped, searched, and questioned
by law enforcement often.
Because he had spent twelve years
in state prison, when the officers
fed his name into their computers
his long rap-sheet was there
exposing all of the crimes he was
convicted of.   Drug dealing was
the bulk of the charges, but petty
theft and minor crimes had been
mounting up since his youth.

The problem of not having
identification was a large hurdle
which had to be addressed.   And
the artist, turned altruist, decided
this was now his mission in life.
He was just the man who could
help make these two street-people
change their lives for the better.   A
lofty goal indeed!   He set about
doing just that.   He made a time to
pick them up and take them to the
DMV to achieve this seemingly
simple task for the two.   When he
got there with them he discovered
that James suffered with a lifelong
learning disability.   He had never
learned to read or write.   Therefore
filling out applications for the state
ID was impossible.   The artist had
to fill out the forms for them.   A
daunting feat at the very least!

After spending the time to complete the paperwork, they were told that James needed a Social Security card in order to apply for the ID.   I think we can see where this is headed.

With half of the day spent, they loaded back into the car and headed for the Social Security office.

After a typically lengthy wait to hear your number called to be served, they were informed that James had to have a copy of his birth certificate before he could begin the process. Ok, let's think about this just for a short minute. Is there a flaw in the bureaucratic system that we all are subject to in our daily lives?   Those of us have lived our whole lives in a white man's world of privilege and immunity have never had to deal with this "catch 22" reality.

Our determined artist spent much time and effort writing to East St. Louis, Illinois requesting a birth certificate for James Adams. Now the waiting game began. Surprisingly, about two weeks later the copy came in the form of a card.   Obtaining housing for James and his honey Robin, was beginning to be questionable in everyone's mind.   An iffy proposition at best!

CHAPTER FIVE: THE NEXT STEP

With card in hand our motley crew headed back to the Social Security office.   After several months and extreme effort spent, James Adams held in his hot-little-hand three necessary items of identification witch he had never possessed in his fifty plus years.   These three forms if ID were typically in every white man's possession since their teenage years.   A birth certificate, a Social Security card, and a drivers' license, all three are part of a sixteen year old kid's "important papers".   With a social security card and a driver's license one can open a bank account, enroll in college, and do damned nearly and thing they want to in this country.

With a huge sigh of relief, James Adams was beginning his new endeavor.   A whole new life of legal wages and being a respectable, tax paying citizen of these United States.   Against all odds this middle aged man with skin of black was starting out on a life much like most folks do in their teens.   At least most white folks.   But remember this whole undertaking began with the goal of obtaining safe and warm housing that James and Robin could claim as their own home. Together, with a warm bed and a kitchen of their own, and a bathroom, and a couch and TV, with the safety of sleeping behind a

locked door.   While it a true fact
that in my crazy years, or at least
crazier than now years, I was
awaken by the brightest light I had
ever seen shining in my eyes and a
deep, Barry White, voice saying
"Son, you had best get your ass up
off of this sidewalk and head out to
your car.   The last person we
found sleeping on this sidewalk had
his throat cut".   That was my first
and last trip to Virginia Beach at
two o'clock in the morning!
Point being, I have never been a
victim of homelessness in any
shape, form, or fashion.
So in order to achieve the reality of
said "housing", James had to have a
job with wages high enough to
afford him that luxury.   Again
robin had a social security check

monthly that was less than a thousand dollars a month.   This amounted to "lunch money" for two people.   However, with a decent pay check weekly for James, they should be able to find some kind of housing.

CHAPTER SIX: THE MAJOR CHALLENGE

Now that James had his Social Security card, he could apply for SSI Disability payments. He again needed his friend and white skin savior to help him through the process of filling out paperwork and to study the rules and requirements. The artist was again ready and more than willing to take up the mantle. After much hard work and time, James was approved and began to receive $740.00 per month. This, along with Robin's $940.00 per month, they had an income base that allowed them to search for housing. Somehow they

were able to continue their life on the streets and stay somewhat healthy.   But time had come to begin the hard work of finding adequate shelter of their own
By this time James had been clean for seven years.   He had not been arrested once for any reason.   This alone should help them in their search.   While the $1680.00 per month was a solid form of income, the timing of the payments would determine at which point in the month they would have enough money to pay the upfront cost required to move in.   And the reality of buying food and incidentals leaves less available cash for housing.   It is much easier to "budget" a large amount of money than a meager amount!   But one

must admit that James and Robins
were people with great fortitude
and courage to have survived the
life they had lived to this point in
time.

They finally found an old motel
that would accept a felon and his
lady with disabilities and "on" SSI
for a monthly charge of $860.00 per
month.   One room, furnished with
a bed, a bathroom and heat and
water, was like heaven for them!
This was a great relief and a
monumental success for people of
their station in life, much to the
credit of their guardian angle on
earth.   The amount of money left
over after paying their monthly rent
was obviously not enough for food
and the basic necessities for two
people.   How can two people buy

food and personal hygiene needs
for a month, out of $820.00
without a kitchen? Fast food and
supermarket prepared "Deli" food
is all they had to choose from.
That's $205.00 per week for two, or
$30.00 each.   It was plain to see
that James had to find part-time
employment.

CHAPTER SEVEN: THE JOB SEARCH

Our tenacious Irish artist friend 'just happened' to know the local Pub owners. One of the jobs in the restaurant business that is difficult to fill and keep good quality employees is dishwasher. Being necessary in order to maintain day to day activities and pass the board of health inspections, owners are always on the lookout for anyone willing to do this menial task. James had worked in the prison kitchen and had tons of dishwashing experience.   The standards in the kitchen were very high.   Food borne illnesses are not desirable in a

state prison and very much frowned
upon by the Warden!

So this indeed seemed like a logical
place to start the job search.   They
set out with resume in hand and
business cards that our artist had
designed and printed for James.
Undoubtedly he was the first
ex-con in history to have not only a
written resume, but also business
cards. One of the pub managers
gave James a shot.   He was offered
eighteen hours per week to begin
with.   He, on the sage advice of his
'job coach', accepted the position.
Granted the wages of a part-time
dishwasher in a pub are not all that
great, it would serve as a start
toward James's new found career.
Any money would be a great help.

James religiously rode his trusty bicycle to and from work every day that he was scheduled. He became a loyal and trusted employee. The manager, after a few months, decided to train James to cook. It turned out to be an effort in futility. Not being able to read the orders was an obvious problem from the get-go. James was not one to feel defeat. Failure to him was not a deterrent. His learned 'nature' from years on the street had hardened him in a good way. As the months passed the manager gained more and more trust in James's character. He decided to take a leap of faith and promote James to the position of "Night Custodian". This job carried a great deal of responsibility. James would be given a set of keys to the backdoor.   He would begin his work at closing time and work every night until four a.m. He would be alone and would have to 'lock-up' when he left.   That's is a heavy load for someone of his past.   He did well and made his bosses proud!   His 'job coach' gave him much well deserved praise and stayed in close touch.

CHAPTER EIGHT:
THE FIRST GLICH

Living in the motel was beginning to be a little restrained for two people in one room and being located on an old highway in the older part of town.   James, being a naturally cordial and debonair man, had friends who loved to visit him when he was off duty.   They enjoyed congregating and sharing lies and yarns of bullshit.   Much the same as most of us.   This attracted the attention of the motel management who apparently asked the police to monitor the situation.   Too many people hanging out at the picnic tables and common areas, sends warning signs of possible illicit activities. James was an early-riser and liked to go out to the table and smoke his first of the day.   A friend or two would join for a smoke and good-morning conversation.   Sometimes the laughter would elevate above the acceptable level. A neighbor across the alley yelled out one morning, "Shut up you fucking nigger!" this did not help his cause.   Anyway, it's hard to have a good time during the day at a cheap motel.   It disturbs the day- sleep of the hookers and pimps. And let's face it, they are the people who slip the managers an occasional Benjamin.   Money talks and bullshit walks!

God I hate to think about the possibility of being "dropped-off"

in the middle of downtown Detroit,
dressed in my red and green plaid
pants and Izod shirt. With no ID
or credit cards. I never carry cash.
 It shivers my timbers!
As you may have discerned, "good
time Charlie" was asked to find
another place to have his daytime
fun. Moving out, of course,
slammed the brakes on James's goal
of, "becoming a respectable citizen"
of a small city which was
ninety-nine percent white folk.
But like water running off of a
ducks back, he mustered all of his
where-with-all, packed his bags and
hit the street, Robin right behind
him all the way. A man's gotta do
what a man's gotta do. Along the
way prior, his counsellor and
costume advisor had strongly

suggested that James drop the dew
rags, the baggy shorts, gang colors,
and backwards ball caps.

Otherwise he probably would never
blend in with whitey.   Changing his
lifestyle would require him to act,
think, and dress like a common
every day person.   Mumbling and
grumbling, James slowly changed
his outward appearance.   This was
one hell of an adjustment for a city
street boy.

He and Robin made the rounds to
the motels with no success.   They
were either denied based on their
appearance or the prices they were
quoted were prohibitive.   Four
hundred a week would not work on
their combined income.   So their
much trusted friend came back into
their lives to help find housing.

James and Robin were spoiled to the "good life" of having a roof over their heads and a soft bed to fall into every night.   And, who isn't?   The serious search began. They decided to move into a motel which charged four hundred a week just to get off of the street.   They would have to diligently watch and check every possibility for shelter which would not eat up their entire income.   James's "extra" income usually was near eight hundred a month.   So that is what they had to survive on.   The "Brainiac" of the trio did his research and made a list of possibilities.   Reading and writing all of the way.   Having no luck after exhausting most of the list, because of James's rap sheet and notorious past, they trudged on

through the darkness.   The
apartment managers made James
pay forty dollars up front to run a
background check.   And he was
not privy to the results of the test,
just the decision of the personnel.
The trusting helper hired an
attorney to draw up a contract that
he could sign as a co-signer.   It was
no help.   After three months of
being dejected, detected, and
neglected time after time, everyone
began to get serious.   They all
started praying.   "Lord have mercy
on we who are truth-tellers and
street dwellers."   "Hard working,
non-shirking, God loving, baby
kissing, dish washing, floor
mopping, non-dealing,
freewheeling, needy homeless
wanderers.   AMEN".

And, low and behold, the next day they found an apartment complex that had a black skin man serving as manager.   A brother of few in the city. He was accommodating and understanding.   He showed mercy on James and Robin.   The apartment was close enough to James's work place to ride his bicycle to and from.   With a little money help from their Irish good luck charm, they pooled enough to pay the man.   So after three long weary months on the streets and in the shelters, they signed the contract and moved into their first apartment ever.   Finally a real home!

CHAPTER NINE: THE NEXT GLITCH

James and Robin enjoyed their new found liberty. James dutifully performed his real job with continued positive reinforcement. Being on time and keeping the establishment clean and sanitary for all patrons and occasional walk-in customers. He loved his job and the affirmation he received. It was a much needed, well deserved, great uplifting of his self-esteem. He wore it on his smile like a badge of honor. He never complained or made excuses for any mistake he may have made. He never took a sick day or left early without

permission.   He truly was a model
employee.

One morning James got a rare call
from his manager.   Now due to all
of the persecution, prosecution, and
dissolution, hardworking James has
suffered in his life, he remains an
unassuming soul. Though he was
puzzled as answered the call, he was
not thinking he had done anything
wrong the night before.   What his
boss had to tell him was a
devastating blow to his physique
and his wellbeing.   No, he was not
fired, but he was definitely out of a
job. He just fell into his chair and
for the first time in many years, he
began to cry.   Robin tried to
console him to no avail.   He finally
regained his composure and
explained his sadness.   His

manager had called to inform him
not to come to work that evening.
There had been an early morning
electrical fire which would cause
them to shut down for an
indeterminate period of time for
repair.
James knew he had to let his best
and only white friend, in the whole
wide world, know this daunting
news.   He wiped his eyes and nose
and went outside for a walk in the
brisk morning air.   The sun was
brightly shinning which did help to
lift his spirits somewhat.   He
walked around the complex and
back home and solemnly took out
his cell.   He pushed the button and
sighed a huge sigh of relief when
his buddy answered.   There was
complete silence after he told in

detail the story of how he lost his only, and best ever, job. After a brief interlude, his confidant and counselor began to so the right thing for that moment. He quietly shed a tear and cleared his throat. He said, "Well, James, you know we have worked through some very difficult problems together thus far, and I'm totally confident that together we will make it through this situation. At least you have a clean, dry, safe home now and I'm sure we will overcome this obstacle. There are other jobs out there, we just have to find one!" He continued, "Everyone has down times and bad luck, we just need to figure out how to put a little more space between the bad ones you are expiring." He said his goodbyes and fell into his chair sobbing.

CHAPTER TEN: BACK TO THE SEARCH

The ever loving unselfish philanthropist, soon got to work on finding James a new job.   He updated the resume and business card and they commenced to 'scrape bell bottoms'.   The new business card had James's name and phone number and the slogan 'will do the work no one else will and I show up'.   James was delighted with his new cards and the quite clever slogan his ingenious friend had come up with.   He was now confident that together they would work this whole job thing out.

They had done it once before and goddamn it they could do it again! After walking in and talking to many owners and managers of eating establishments, they found him a dishwashing position.   This was a larger restaurant with a faster moving and more demanding kitchen situation.   There were several Chefs and waiters and waitresses and they all evidently were James's boss.   At least they all thought they were.   Now I ain't saying that there was an element of racism involved in all of the shouting and yelling taking place, but a young Chef always called him "BOY!" when he addressed him. James explained that he was insulted by being call 'boy' and please not do it anymore. Of course that fell on deaf ears. James was fifty-five by this time and his body was riddled with scars from knife fights on the streets of the cities in his earlier days. The bullet lodged in his left leg made it hard to shuffle back and forth as he operated the large commercial dishwashing machine. His arthritic 'old bones' were sore way before their time. Twelve years of prison life will do that to a person. The pace in the kitchen of the prison did not move so fast. Certainly much slower than his new job required. In order to run thousands of people in and out of a large restaurant, everyone's every move has to be fast and furious.

It's constant 'hustle and bustle' in flurry and flash. In this case, speed equals MONEY! James could not keep up with all of the young bucks he competed with on an everyday basis. Yes, he was asked to resign after only two weeks of total hell.

His trusted guiding force quietly explained, "This is not surprising to me, it happens to almost everyone at some time in their life." These are most definitely true words of wisdom for us all to live by. I mean, you know, who among us has not been "let go" from at least one or two positions of high community standing. Let me see a show of hands! OK then!

Back to the search we go once again.   For all involved, this was beginning to feel like being trapped on a merry-go-round, kind of like trying to out run the blade of a lawn mower, a little bit like trying to swim to that next buoy that is floating out with the tide. Our lowly local hero buckled his seat belt once again and loaded his car with James and his lovely fiancée Robin and head out to the suburbs looking for permanent employment.   This time in a smaller eatery or pup. They needed that extra money to supplement their solid income.   They were not in fear of losing their home, but a little bit of spending change would come in handy.   Without it their

"money was funny and their change
was strange!"

CHAPTER ELEVEN: WHAT THE HELL

Listen to this, James comes home one day during his 'job hunt' and gets his mail as he walks in the door.   You will not believe this! He got a nice form letter from the Social Security Administration telling him he is making too much money in his part time work. James had worked at the Washington State fair for four weeks after he was let go from his restaurant job. Evidently this income, because the paperwork lag time in forms submitted, was assumed to be 'on-top-of' his restaurant job. WHAT?   His local wages ran around $185.00 per month!   OK, let's add this up. $185.00 plus his $740.00 per month from SSI. WHAT?   When I was a child I remember the 'sages of the ages' saying, "If you give people 'wellfare' money, they will not go out and look for a job."   Where is the logic in that?   I consider this a 'test case' one 'for the books'. Do "they" want people on the streets? So here they go back to the Social Security office. It is always fun to meet with the intelligency.

Our fearless leader told James to "dress to impress" for the meeting because it was really important. When he picked them up for the appointment he was a bit taken aback. To say the least. Brother James was dressed in his city finest.

He wore his creased loose fitting khaki pants and his black silk shirt buttoned to the top.   Accessorized with a stylish gold chain necklace with a cross of David hanging just below the top button.   And, his black patent leather, smooth toe "shiny French shoes", and his long black trench coat.   Topped off with his flawless black fedora.   'LAWD HAVE MERCY'! Dressed to kill! If we only had a photograph for posterity!   The man was truly a dandy!

Well, when the meeting began James sat down in front of the social worker with his charming, larger than life personality, his huge laugh and his big white toothy smile and said, "You remind me of my sister."   Her response was "Your

sister must be a beautiful lady."
We all roared with light hearted,
genuine laughter.   The meeting
went very smoothly. His "ice
breaker" was a big hit for all and
came quite naturally. The man is a
'pip'! Since then the problems with
SSI have been "worked out"!

CHAPTER TWELVE: MEANWHILE

During the time that James was working at his first restaurant job and doing well financially, his friend and teacher got a call from him saying he needed a ride to the emergency room.   Robin was feeling ill.   They helped her into the car and to the hospital.   After an hour or two, a doctor came and explained what was going on with Robin's health.   He explained to them that she had multiple problems, including schizophrenia, diabetes, being overweight, and she had a 'blown hip'.   He told them he could only treat the problems that he could, and get Robin back home. He could not address all of her issues!

Ultimately, as if James needed more to deal with in his life, Robin had to have a hip replacement operation. While she was in the hospital, a Psychiatrist came and gave her a thorough examination. He informed James that he had two fiancées. He called them Robin one and Robin two. The disabilities that Robin suffered from were caused by problems at birth, abuse by males, and past drug abuse. It all began to "fall-in-place" for James. During the time they had been together some days Robin behaved as the lady he dearly loved and knew well, and other days she was a complete stranger.

Robin two had applied for a credit card on one of those applications sent to everyone as 'junk mail'. Who knows how she was approved, but she got her card?   Not being financially savvy, she went on a spending spree and built up a huge debt.   If Robin one was around when the monthly payment was due she paid it.   However if Robin two was there, she blew it off.   The card was cancelled by the bank for nonpayment and went into "collection". James and his 'guiding friend' found out when he attempted to move to a different apartment.   The credit check was rejected because of her outstanding debt.   I know, what the hell is

wrong with this system?   Maybe
'banking scam"?   James decided he
wanted to clear the bad debt that
Robin two had incurred.   With the
help of his good personal friend, he
contacted the bank and worked out
a payment plan that he could
handle.   Life for James was
anything but boring!
The operation that the "Robins"
had to have was quite an ordeal.
Due to their finances, the Doctor
informed them that she had to
leave the hospital the same day of
the operation.   This presented a
monumental challenge for someone
who only has a bicycle as their
mode of transportation.   An
ambulance brought them to their
apartment building and the driver
helped them to the sidewalk in

front of their unit.   He wished them luck and drove away.   Their apartment was on the third floor and there was no elevator.   The Robins weighed 250 pounds at that time.   James was told that maybe the fire department would help him get her up to their apartment.   He called and they came. They finally got her into their apartment. James was tired and confused about the care and rehabilitation process they had in front of them.   The next day he called his artist friend and explained he was not up to the task and that he was leaving her there to take care of herself the best she could.   After some counseling and consoling James agreed to stay and try to help her recover.   Slowly together they progressed and she is doing as well as can be expected.   Robin and James had been together fifteen years at that time.   He did the right thing and 'stuck it out'.

 They became aware of a "caregiver" assistance program that they could apply for.   Technically, they met the qualifications needed for the help.   James had been a hardworking, law abiding citizen of the community for eight years by then.   So the three of them together completed hours of the proper paperwork and submitted it by taking it into the office.   The program administrators reviewed and perused all of the paperwork. They also did a background check as a matter of requirement.   A dubious committee decided they must reject the application due to James's notorious past history. Please, charity has its limits!   If free caregiving money is given to a man who, paid his dues in prison for twelve horrific years, had a "come to Jesus moment" and completely changed his behavior for the better, straightened out his life, took on the care and protection of a street wandering mentally ill lady of poor health, and became a well-respected, tax paying citizen; then how can tell our Mayor and County and State Judges that we have diligently doled out the white tax payers of county and state property taxes, that we have properly appropriated the meager budget allocated for the purpose of helping the meekest, flawless, and weakest among us?   How can we keep our upstanding position in our lovely little county?!   People like "this" should move into the core of Seattle!

CHAPTER THIRTEEN: THE GREAT APPEAL

Guess what!   The organization actually had an appeals process available.   And yes, it only requires a mountain of paperwork and a meeting with a Judge, the agency personnel, and our three, quickly becoming community rebel rousers.   They established a meeting time and went about their lives.   When the day finally came for their "meeting", due to the Covid Virus, it ended up being a four-way teleconference.   There was the Judge, three state employees, and James, his recovering lovely ladies Robin one and Robin two, and their loving friend with "God on his side". Eight personalities from worlds so far apart that it was like they were speaking in eight different tongues.

Trying to have a meaningful dialogue was ludicrous to say the least!   Needless to say, the outcome of the 'meeting' was predictable. James's trusted 'sit-in' attorney, had done his homework.   He watched 'PERRY MASON' religiously every day for months. He presented 'Exhibit A-1' to start the conservation.   He expounded and expatiated on how his 'client and dear black friend' had paid the price of the sin against society of selling and using "drugs", for twelve long, hard years.   Hell that was twenty years ago and anyway, the past is

past!   He declared that James
needed a well-deserved
"expungement" of his record, of
one man's life of crime.
While he had the 'floor' he
continued to explain how that
James was determined to continue
living his life as straight as an arrow,
the same way he had for the last,
almost, ten years.   And to be an
upright, forthright without evasion,
tax paying, bill paying, dragon
slaying, citizen of his new found
and beloved home town and
community.   How that James and
the Robins were not only 'walking
the high road', they were just not
hurting one damned single solitary
human being.   They were church
going and clean spitting, soft talking
and slow walking, shower taking

and soul searching, one of those people who always makes a good neighbor in any subdivision.   Of course the Judge was especially impress with this 'lawyer show watching', retired school teacher who loved to do his dead level best, to save as many people in need as he possibly could in his remaining time on the face of this old globe, spinning out of control.

As to be expected, the bureaucrats came with a pile of folders full of regulations and stipulations regarding this particular case. They were armed 'to-the teeth'. They had lead in their pistols. They spewed WAC codes and principles.   They spoke words of rule and proper behavior.   Basically speaking, they were "hard asses".

The Judge seemed to be somewhat sympathetic to their cause but in true fashion, notwithstanding James's counselor's feeble attempt at replicating Perry Mason.
His closing argument was that former inmates deserved an opportunity to redeem and improve themselves. And to transform their lives. James had done that. The judge would not allow the presentation of "Exhibit B" which was signed letters of recommendation from James's previous bosses attesting to his high character, his excellent attitude and beautiful work ethic, and trustworthy demeanor. For some weird reason the Judge thought the letters needed to be notarized affidavits. The gavel dropped.

Case closed!   What's for lunch?
Total disqualification soon followed
via of mail a while later.   The
troopers still have one appeal left.
And you can damned well bet they
will use. It.   They have decided to
contact the pro-bono attorneys that
the Judge recommended and
explain their plight.   As it should
be! After the meeting was over,
James said "Wow, I usually have a
front row seat in situations like this,
but today I was in the back row."

CHAPTER FOURTEEN: FROM HERE TO ETERNITY

OK! James decided to better his life, while conducting his job search, by taking reading lessons. He found a Puyallup Valley self-improvement organization that offers reading classes. James has a private tutor who works closely with him.   These volunteers are usually retired school teachers and are very 'good at what they do'. He has had three lessons so far. He may never sit down and read a novel, but as long as he can read and write enough to fill out forms, it will be will be a great help.   He does desire to improve his status in life.   Not being able to read and write is very frustrating and debilitating for anyone and much more common than most of us realize.   These people, by-in-large, are people of other skin color than white.   There are however, thousands of people with white skin who are living on the streets and in inner cities, and in very rural areas of these United States, who are illiterate.   These people have learned to live with this huge disability by taking menial jobs that they learn by watching and mimicking others.   Custodial and dishwashing, auto detailing and auto body jobs.   To name a few. They learn to count money and to sign their name and that becomes the extent of their literary skills. Many of these people receive a high school diploma or "certificate of attendance". They actually complete twelve years of public school.

James found a job at a large grocery chain store. His responsibilities included sanitizing and performing custodial work. His trusty helping 'soldier of goodness', spent several hours online doing the application process. James would in no way have been able to do that on his own. Much to their amazement, the background check apparently came back OK. Hallelujah! He is doing well in his present position. He has an effervescent personality and people love him. They enjoy his big toothy smile and overwhelming presence.   He flatters and flirts and does his job extremely well.   He never misses a day and never pisses and moans about his duties.   He happily fills his hours at work doing his job without conflict or discussion.   An example of the perfect employee. Every employers dream!

CHAPTER FIFTEEN: LASTING HOPE

This fictional account of a sixty year old black skin man who is living at this time in space, leads me to believe that in this Whiteman's World, everyone else is living way beneath their dignity, and their station in life is demeaned and diminished.   They exist in a world of gloam and gloom.   They strive each and every day to keep their "head above water".   They struggle to keep food on the table and shelter over their heads.   They do the "dirty work" that no one else will do.   They clean the shitters and urinals, and the showers and

tile floors.   They wash the dishes
and wipe the tables and they sweep
and vacuum and mop the floors.
They wipe vomit up off of the floor
and disinfect all of the surfaces that
they clean with harsh chemicals that
most of us will never come in
contact with.

James is still working in the grocery
store and doing quite well, thank
you very much!   He is well
appreciated by management, fellow
employees, and customers alike.
He does not miss work for any
reason.   He arrives early and leaves
late.   He does his assigned duties
and goes above and beyond what is
expected of him.   He has been
"straight" in the eyes of the "law",
in the great state of Washington
since March 12, 1998.   He was

arrested for selling marijuana.   He
again had an arrest in June of 2013
for the same offence.   As we all
know, recreational use of marijuana
is legal in Washington State now
and has been for several years.   Yet
this man of black skin is still being
prosecuted for these crimes.   His
record must be expunged of these
and other related crimes he was
arrested for in his past life.
Desperate people do desperate
deeds in order to survive.   Survival
on the streets is not only the worst
way to live ones' life, but the easiest
and quickest way to ones' death.
The poorest among us, the
wretched and the lonely, the love-
lost and the homely, the addict and
the user, the drunkard and the
poseur, the wanderer and the

runner, the shooter and the gunner,
the mentally ill and the PTSD, the
dyslexic and the OCD, the psalmist
and writer, the sick and the fighter,
walking dead and the screamer, the
marcher and the dreamer, the
sleeper and the stalker, the bleeder
and the walker.
The meek shall inherit eternity!
The strong shall pay eternally!